I am an Amazing Asian girl

A Positive Affirmation Book for Asian Girls

ILLUSTRATED BY
Jade Le

WRITTEN BY
Yobe Qiu

All inquiries including bulk purchase for promotional, educational, and business events, should be directed to
hello@byyobeqiu.com

Published in U.S.A by By Yobe Qiu, LLC 2022

ISBN: 978-1-957711-02-7 (Paperback)
ISBN: 978-1-957711-03-4 (Hardback)

Book cover design and illustrations by Jade Le

Dedicated

To BaBa, Thank you for always making me feel valued, special and powerful. Your Little Girl

I am an Amazing Asian Girl,
My grandparents tell me so.

I am not afraid to shine,
I am my ancestors' pride, I am divine!

I am an Adaptable Asian Girl,
My parents tell me so.
I am ready to conquer any challenges, I can go with the flow.
I can work with any situation, that I know!

I'm an Accomplished Asian Girl.
My teachers tell me so.

Chiaki Mukai

Who is the first Asian woman in space?

I will try to give my very best
when I am facing any test!

I am an Active Asian Girl.
My coaches tell me so.

I love adventures and love the twirls.
I can wear a helmet as I take on the world!

I am an Appreciated Asian Girl.
My friends tell me so.
I do not need to compete for love, attention or praise.
I know I am valued even when it's shown in different ways!

I am an Assertive Asian Girl.
My siblings tell me so.

I have my own thoughts. I paint my path with my own color.
I have a voice that I speak with purpose, pride and power!

I am an Authentic Asian Girl.
My classmates tell me so.

itadakimasu!

I am proud of my identity
and my culture too.

I embrace my traditions
in everything I do!

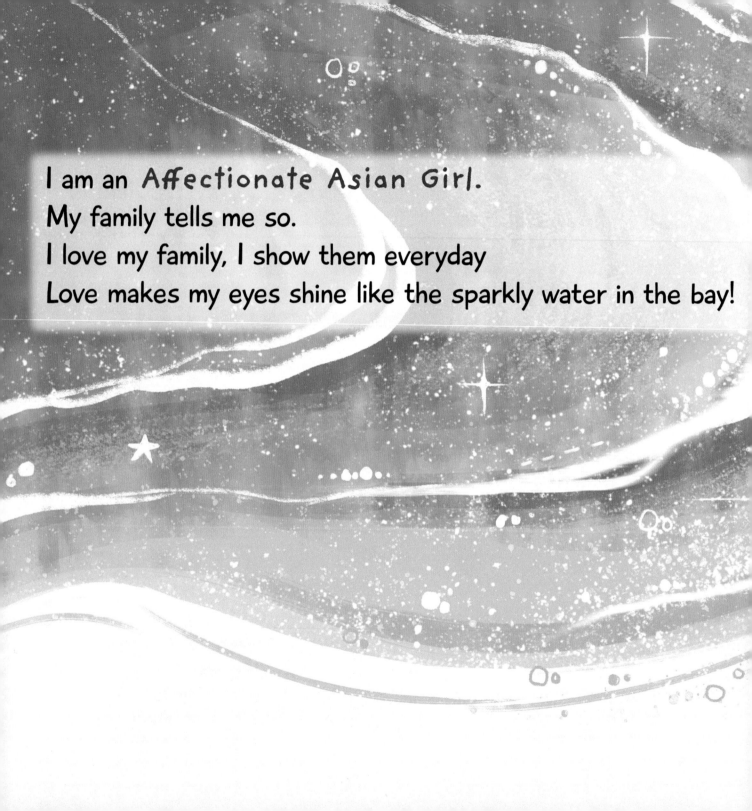

I am an Affectionate Asian Girl.
My family tells me so.
I love my family, I show them everyday
Love makes my eyes shine like the sparkly water in the bay!

I am adaptable, accomplished, active, appreciated, assertive, authentic, affectionate and amazing.
I'm all of these and more!

I am an Amazing Asian Girl.
I tell myself so.

Jade is a Vietnamese artist who works as a full-time freelance illustrator in Singapore. Her love for drawing began as a hobby and gradually evolved into a blooming career. One of her greatest joys is assisting inspired authors to present their engaging stories in beautiful artworks. When she has free time, Jade draws inspiration from everyday life. She hopes you will enjoy her work as much as she has fun illustrating it.

 jaesthetic.studio@gmail.com   www.jaesthetic.art

Illustrator

Yobe Qiu is an educator, entrepreneur, mom, and bestselling author with a passion for storytelling. As an educator, Yobe taught children and their families to embrace love and diverse cultures. When she identified a need for more multicultural books, she decided to create her own children's stories featuring Asian characters and cultures. Today, Yobe is proud to publish books that help children like her daughter feel seen, heard, and represented. Yobe looks forward to writing many more stories in the years to come.

Author

 hello@byyobeqiu.com   www.byyobeqiu.com

OTHER TITLES BY YOBE QIU

» Our Lunar New Year

» Our Moon Festival

» Our Double Fifth Celebration

» The Asian Holidays Children's Activity Book

» Asian Adventures A-Z

If you enjoyed this book, or any of Yobe Qiu's books, please leave a review. Your kindness and support are greatly appreciated!